TRIANGLES
PYRAMIDS & CONES

PETER PATILLA

BELITHA PRESS

First published in Great Britain in 1994 by

Belitha Press Limited
31 Newington Green, London N16 9PU

Text copyright © Peter Patilla 1994

Format and illustrations copyright © Belitha Press Ltd 1994

Printed in Hong Kong for Imago

ISBN 1 85561 273 9 (hardback)
ISBN 1 85561 330 1 (paperback)

British Library Cataloguing in Publication Data CIP data for this book is available from the British Library

Acknowledgements

Photographic credits: J.Allen Cash Photo Library: pages 23 (top left), 25 (bottom); Tony Buckley: pages 4–5; Robert Harding Picture Library: pages 12 (top right), 19 (bottom), 22 (bottom left), 24 (centre); Michael Holford: page 8 (bottom); Image Bank, London: pages 11 (bottom right), 12 (top left), 15 (centre right); Mansell Collection: page 22 (top); Tony Stone Worldwide: cover, pages 6 (bottom), 7 (centre and bottom), 14 (bottom), 15 (centre left), 18 (both), 24 (top and bottom), 25 (top right); Zefa Picture Library: pages 15 (bottom), 25 (top left).
All other photographs taken by Claire Paxton
Illustrations: Jonathon Satchell
Mobile and cone models: Deborah Crow
Editor: Rachel Cooke
Designer: John Calvert
Picture researcher: Juliet Duff
Thanks to our models Murriam and Oliver

CONTENTS

WHAT IS A TRIANGLE?

A triangle is a shape that has three straight sides and three corners. Corners of shapes can be called either **angles** or **vertices.** One corner is called a **vertex.**

The word triangle comes from a Latin word: *tri* meaning three and *angulus* meaning angle. Other words to do with three of something begin with *tri* – think of *tri*plets or a musical *tri*o.

All these shapes are triangles.

TRIANGULAR SHAPES

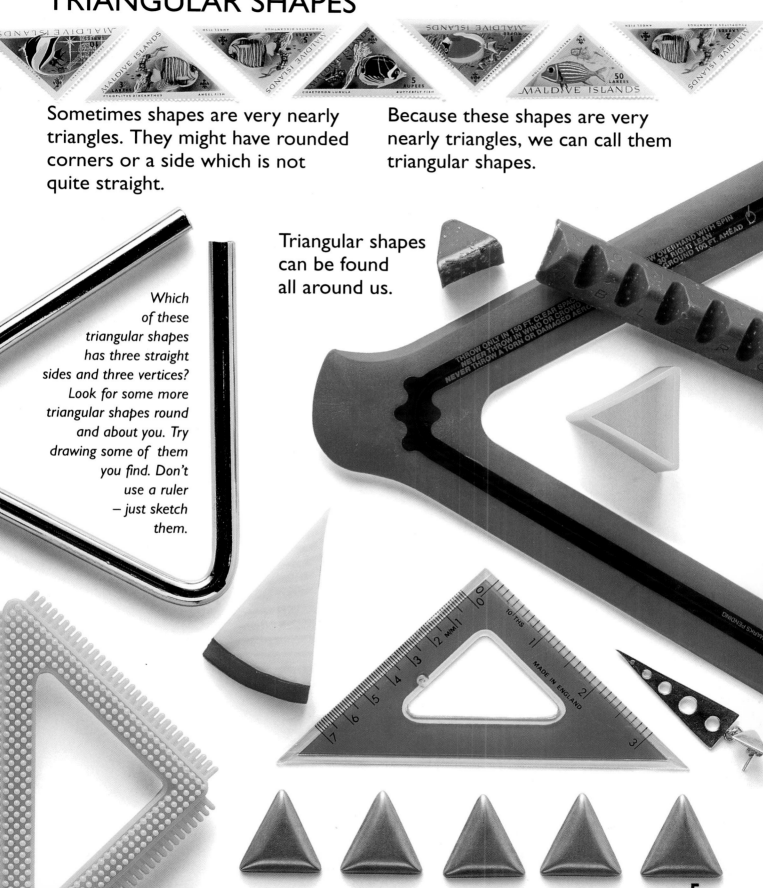

Sometimes shapes are very nearly triangles. They might have rounded corners or a side which is not quite straight.

Because these shapes are very nearly triangles, we can call them triangular shapes.

Triangular shapes can be found all around us.

Which of these triangular shapes has three straight sides and three vertices? Look for some more triangular shapes round and about you. Try drawing some of them you find. Don't use a ruler – just sketch them.

SIDES OF A TRIANGLE

We can group different triangles by the lengths of their sides.

Scalene triangles have no sides which are the same length. None of their angles are the same either. The word scalene comes from a Greek word meaning uneven.

Here are some isosceles triangles.

Some triangles have two sides the same length. They are called **isosceles**. The word isosceles comes from a Greek word meaning equal legs. When two sides are the same length, two angles of the triangle are the same size.

Here are some scalene triangles.

Here are some equilateral triangles.

ISOSCELES AS WELL

An equilateral triangle is also an isosceles triangle. It has two equal sides and two equal angles. What makes it special is that its third side and angle are equal as well.

EQUAL SIDES

Some triangles have all three sides the same length. They are called **equilateral**, from a Latin word meaning equal sided. The three angles are also the same size. How many equilateral and isosceles triangles can you see on these pages?

A tower of equilateral triangles. The triangles become smaller the higher they are in the tower. Notice how they fit neatly on top of each other.

◀ *Lines disappearing into the distance can look like triangles, such as on this road.*

▶ *There are many different triangle shapes to be found in the roof tops of this town in Germany. See what kinds you can spot.*

ANGLES IN TRIANGLES

Every triangle has three angles. The size of the angles can vary. We measure angles by looking at how much of a circle they turn through.

A very important type of angle is called a **right angle**. A right angle is quarter of a complete turn. It is sometimes called a square corner.

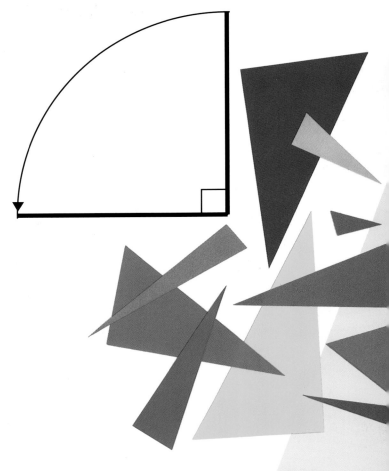

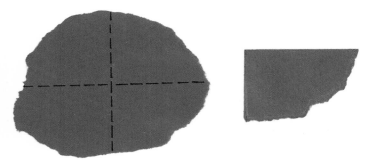

It is easy to make a right angle checker. Fold a piece of paper to make a straight edge. Fold it again so that one part of the straight edge lies exactly along the other part. The corner where the straight edges meet is the right angle.

Here are some right angled triangles. Place the right angle of your checker over each of their vertices to find the right angles.

MEASURING ANGLES

Your right angle checker is one way of measuring angles. Another way is to use a **protractor**. This measures angles in degrees. There are 360 degrees in a complete turn. A quarter turn (that is, a right angle) is 90°. A ° is a short way of writing degrees.

This is an old ship's compass. It measures direction in degrees. How many degrees are there between North and East?

8

Of course, not all triangles have a right angle. Some triangles have all three angles smaller than a right angle. These triangles are called **acute triangles**. The word acute comes from a Latin word which means sharpened.

Here are some acute triangles. Use your right angle checker to see that all the angles are smaller than 90°.

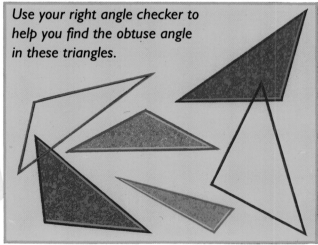

Use your right angle checker to help you find the obtuse angle in these triangles.

Some triangles have one angle which is bigger than a right angle. These triangles are called **obtuse triangles**. The word obtuse comes from a Latin word which means blunt.

ADDING ANGLES TOGETHER
Cut out a paper triangle. Rip off the corners and put them together like this:

The three corners make a straight line or two right angles. This straight line measures 180°. Do you think the angles of any triangle will always make 180° when you add them together? Rip the corners off different sorts of triangles to see.

DRAWING TRIANGLES

You can make all sorts of patterns and designs from triangles, but first you've got to learn how to draw them. There are a few suggestions on this page. See what other ways you can think of.

Try drawing some triangles without using a ruler – just sketch the shapes.

Sketch an equilateral triangle. Measure the sides to see how good you were.

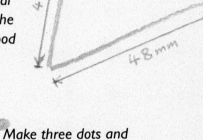

Make three dots and join them together. Try doing this with a ruler as well. Can you draw an isosceles triangle using this method?

USING COMPASSES

You can draw triangles using a pair of compasses and a ruler.

I. *Draw a straight line.*

2. *With the compasses stretched to the length of the line, draw a section of a circle (an arc) as shown.*

3. *Draw an arc from the other end of the line in the same way.*

4. *Join up each end of the line to where the two arcs cross. What sort of triangle have you drawn?*

TRIANGLE PATTERNS

When a shape or pattern can be divided into two parts that reflect each other exactly, it is **symmetrical**.

Cut out a shape from the side of a folded sheet of paper. Open out the paper and look at the hole. The hole will always be symmetrical.

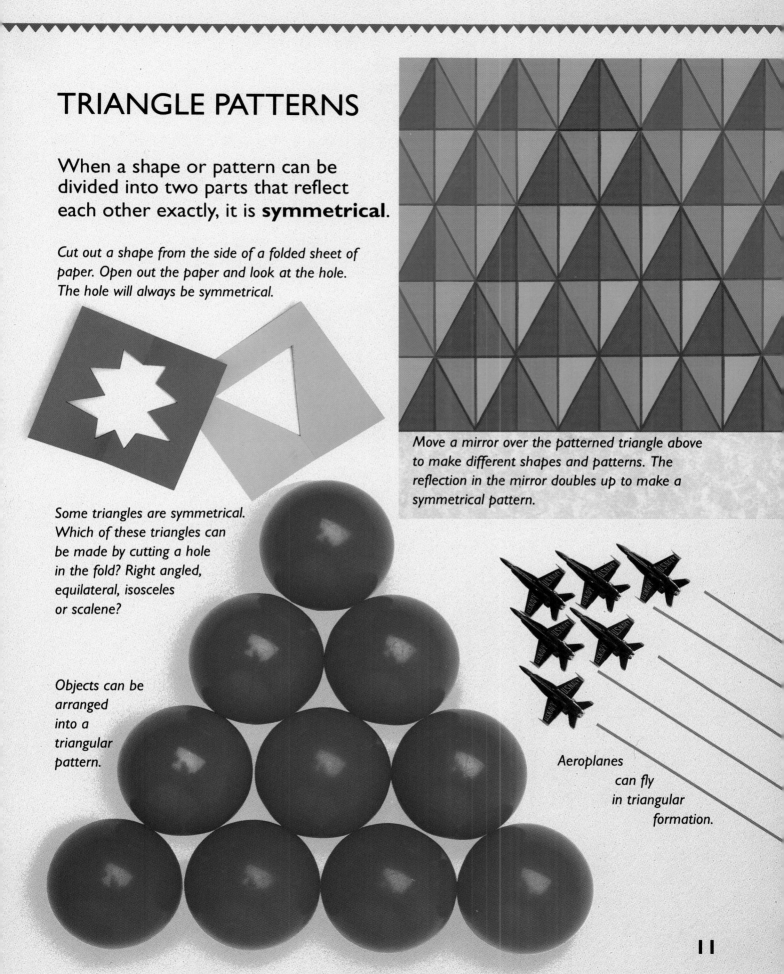

Some triangles are symmetrical. Which of these triangles can be made by cutting a hole in the fold? Right angled, equilateral, isosceles or scalene?

Objects can be arranged into a triangular pattern.

Move a mirror over the patterned triangle above to make different shapes and patterns. The reflection in the mirror doubles up to make a symmetrical pattern.

Aeroplanes can fly in triangular formation.

FITTING TOGETHER

Many different shapes, including triangles, can fit together without leaving any gaps. We call this **tessellation.** The word comes from a Latin word which means square shapes, but you can use other shapes to make a tessellating pattern. The four pictures here are all examples of tessellation.

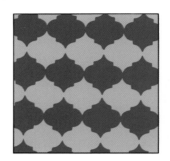

TESSELLATING TRIANGLES
Every triangle will tessellate to make a pattern. Cut a card triangle and draw round it to make your own tessellating pattern.

The triangle panels of an umbrella must tessellate to keep the rain out!

TANGRAMS

A tangram is a square which has been cut into several pieces. It was a puzzle invented over 4000 years ago by the Chinese. It is thought that the name comes from a game played by the Tanka, who lived on boats and traded from Chinese ports. There are several types of tangram but this one is the most famous. It has five triangles, a square and a **parallelogram.**

Make a tangram for yourself. Cut it out of strong card, following the layout shown here.

TANGRAM PICTURES

The seven pieces can be arranged like a jigsaw to make hundreds of different pictures and shapes. They can also be arranged to make a large isosceles triangle.

MAKING NEW SHAPES

You may have already realized with your triangle designs that triangles can fit together to make straight-edged shapes with more than three sides. Any closed shape made from straight lines is called a **polygon**. The word polygon means many angles, although we identify a particular polygon by the number of sides it has. A triangle is a three-sided polygon.

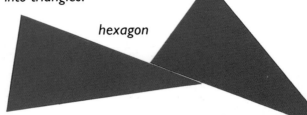

Here are a few polygons. By drawing lines between some vertices of these polygons you can divide them into triangles.

hexagon

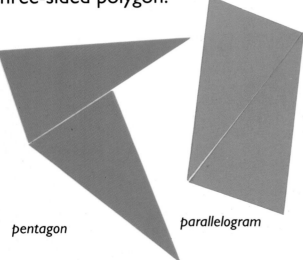

pentagon

parallelogram

Experiment with making new shapes from triangles by cutting out two identical card triangles and fitting them together. Here are some of the shapes you can make and their names.

Apart from triangles, what shapes can you see in these pictures?

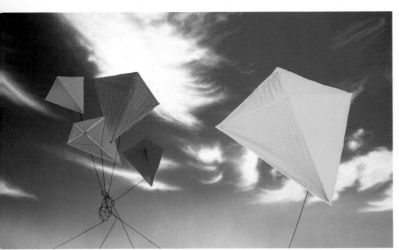

STRONG STRUCTURES

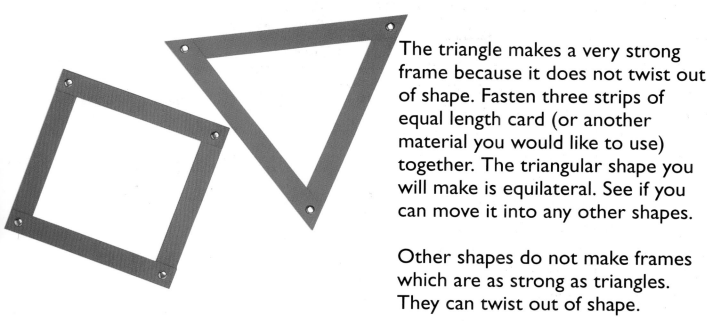

The triangle makes a very strong frame because it does not twist out of shape. Fasten three strips of equal length card (or another material you would like to use) together. The triangular shape you will make is equilateral. See if you can move it into any other shapes.

Other shapes do not make frames which are as strong as triangles. They can twist out of shape.

Here are some strong triangle structures:

◄ The position of this giraffe's legs give it solid support as it bends to drink.

► Pylons need to be very rigid to carry electricity cables safely.

▼ Bridges which span over long distances must be strong.

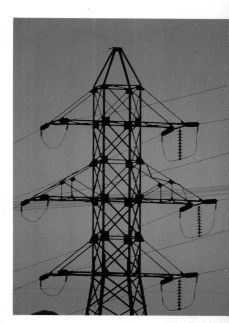

WHAT IS A PYRAMID?

The strong structure of a triangle can be used to make pyramids.

Pyramids are not flat shapes, like triangles, but **three-dimensional** (3-D for short). This means they have depth as well as length and width. A triangle has only length and width. Pyramids each have a polygon at their base. The other faces are triangles which meet at a vertex at the pyramid's top.

*This mobile is made up entirely of different pyramids. Some of them are **skeletal** pyramids. They have been made by straws, which act like the bones of a skeleton. You can see right through each skeletal pyramid.*

16

Sometimes pyramids have their tops cut off. These are called **truncated pyramids.**

Can you see truncated pyramids in this picture?

FROM BUILDINGS TO BOXES

The most famous pyramids of all were built in ancient Egypt in about 2600-2500BC. They were the monuments and burial places for the royal families of Egypt – in particular, their kings who were called pharaohs. The pyramids at Giza still stand today. The largest, the pyramid called Khufu, is 138 m (453 ft) high. It is the only survivor of the 'Seven Wonders of the World'.

Pyramid temples were also built in Central America, by the Mayan people, between AD300 and 900, and later the Aztecs. They were used to worship their sun, moon and rain gods.

The ancient pyramids at Giza.

The entrance to the Louvre Museum in Paris is a modern pyramid built of glass.

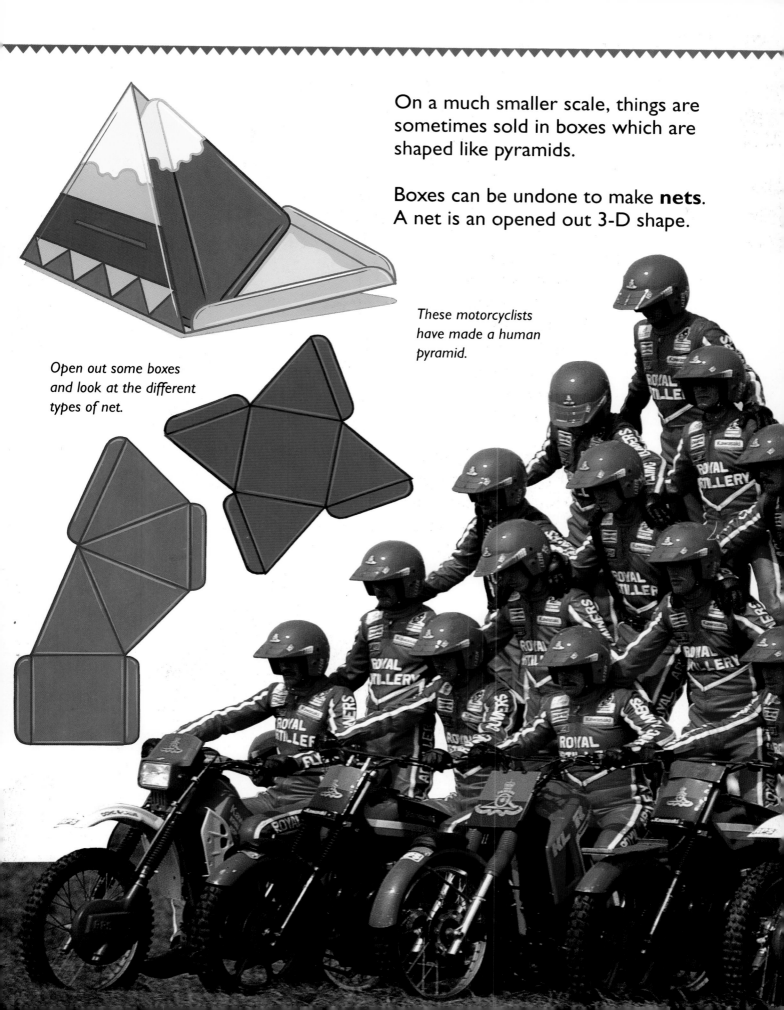

On a much smaller scale, things are sometimes sold in boxes which are shaped like pyramids.

Boxes can be undone to make **nets**. A net is an opened out 3-D shape.

These motorcyclists have made a human pyramid.

Open out some boxes and look at the different types of net.

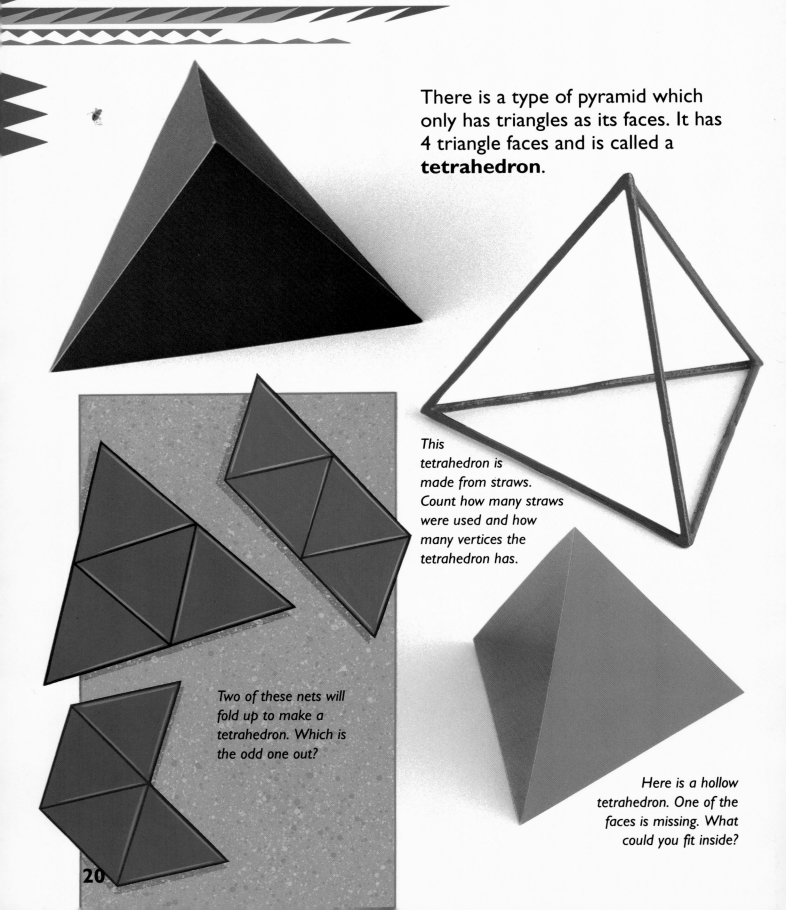

There is a type of pyramid which only has triangles as its faces. It has 4 triangle faces and is called a **tetrahedron**.

This tetrahedron is made from straws. Count how many straws were used and how many vertices the tetrahedron has.

Two of these nets will fold up to make a tetrahedron. Which is the odd one out?

Here is a hollow tetrahedron. One of the faces is missing. What could you fit inside?

20

TETRAHEDRON TROUBLES

Here are two troubling tetrahedron challenges for you to take on. To do them you will need some card, scissors, sticky tape, a ruler, a pencil – and all your wits about you!

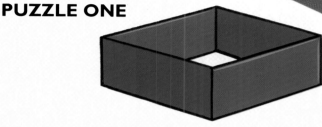

PUZZLE ONE

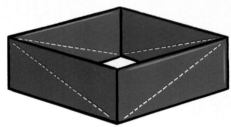

1. Cut out 2 rectangles, each measuring 5 cm by 18 cm.

2. Carefully fold down the middle of each rectangle dividing it along its longest edges.

3. Now fold in the diagonals of each half of the card.

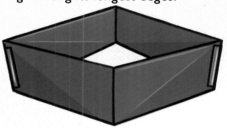

4. Stick the short edges together with some tape. Challenge: fold the card into a tetrahedron.

PUZZLE TWO

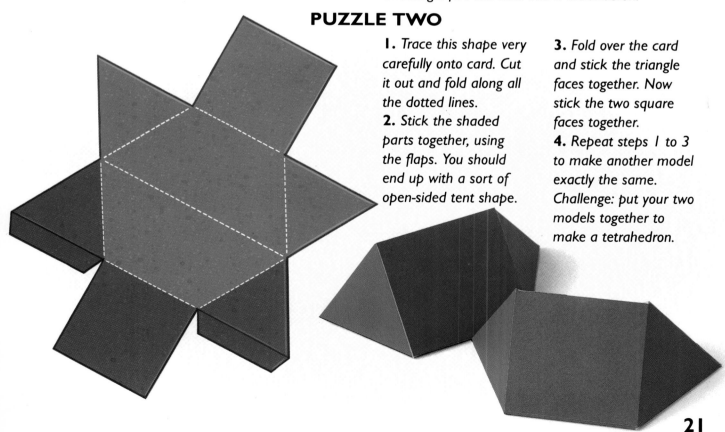

1. Trace this shape very carefully onto card. Cut it out and fold along all the dotted lines.

2. Stick the shaded parts together, using the flaps. You should end up with a sort of open-sided tent shape.

3. Fold over the card and stick the triangle faces together. Now stick the two square faces together.

4. Repeat steps 1 to 3 to make another model exactly the same. Challenge: put your two models together to make a tetrahedron.

PART OF A FAMILY

Pyramids are members of a family of shapes called polyhedra. A single one of these shapes is called a polyhedron. A polyhedron is a solid shape which is made from lots of polygons. The word polyhedron comes from a Greek word meaning many faces.

Which of these polyhedra is a pyramid?

The Epcot Centre in America looks like a golf ball. It is a massive polyhedra made out of triangles.

Polyhedra have flat faces, straight edges and vertices. There is a formula for connecting the number of faces, edges and vertices on a solid. Although other mathematicians knew the formula beforehand, it was a Swiss mathematician called Euler who made it famous. Euler lived between 1707 and 1783.
The formula is:

Vertices + Faces - Edges = 2.

The formula works for any polyhedra.

Vertices + Faces - Edges = 2.
4 + 4 - 6 = 2

Vertices + Faces - Edges = 2.
8 + 6 - 12 = 2

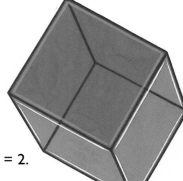

Vertices + Faces - Edges = 2.
5 + 5 - 8 = 2

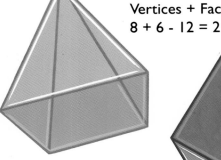

22

WHAT IS A CONE?

A pyramid with many sides can look like a cone. The more sides it has the more cone-like it becomes.

A cone is a three-dimensional shape with a circular base, from which a curved surface comes to a vertex. It is rather like a curved pyramid.

Hollow cones can be useful for holding food. Sometimes you can eat the cone as well!

If you were to cut straight down the middle of a cone from its vertex to its base, the flat face of each half of the cone would be a triangle.

A truncated cone has had the vertex at its top cut off.

23

CONES EVERYWHERE

Cone shapes are all around us. Sometimes they are truncated. Sometimes they are used with other shapes.

Can you spot the cone shapes on these pages? What other uses for a cone can you think of?

Cone shapes can be found in the natural world, like the mushrooms shown here. Can you think of other cone shapes to be found in nature?

MAKING CONES

Make your own card cone and see how many different uses you can think of for it.

1. *Draw a large circle on some card. You can use compasses or draw round something with a circular base. Cut it out.*
2. *Cut a straight line to the centre of the circle.*

3. *Pull one section of the circle across the other along the straight line you have cut.*

This will make a cone shape. The further you pull the sections together, the tighter your cone will be. Choose the cone shape you want and secure it with sticky tape.

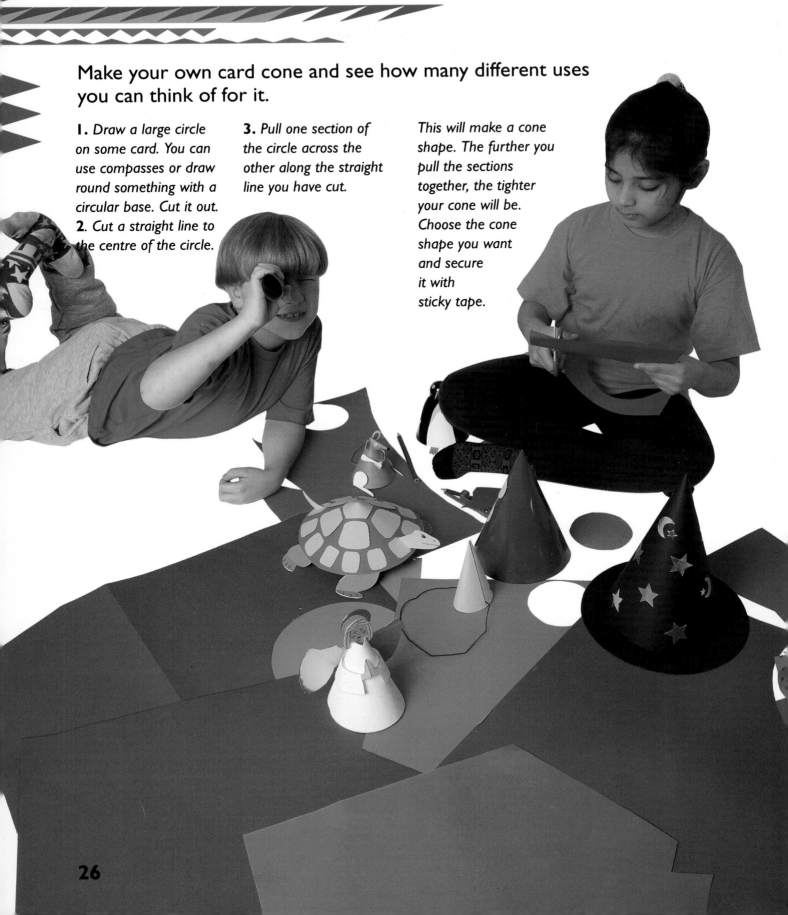

UNUSUAL CONES

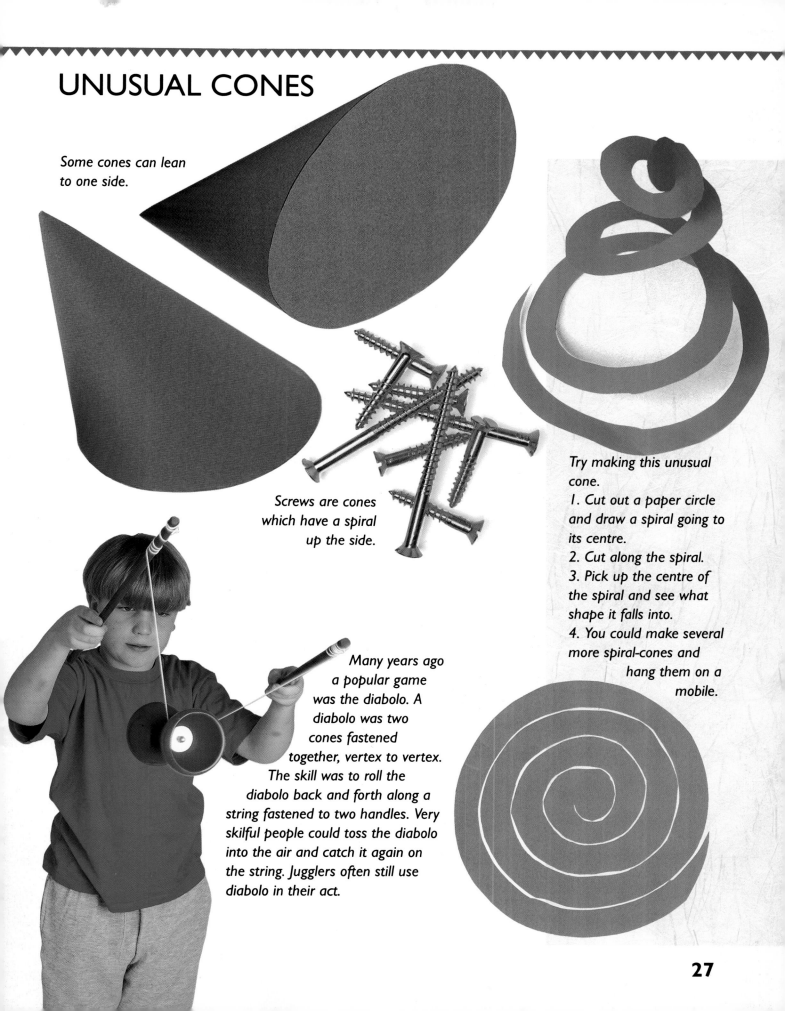

Some cones can lean to one side.

Screws are cones which have a spiral up the side.

Try making this unusual cone.
1. Cut out a paper circle and draw a spiral going to its centre.
2. Cut along the spiral.
3. Pick up the centre of the spiral and see what shape it falls into.
4. You could make several more spiral-cones and hang them on a mobile.

Many years ago a popular game was the diabolo. A diabolo was two cones fastened together, vertex to vertex. The skill was to roll the diabolo back and forth along a string fastened to two handles. Very skilful people could toss the diabolo into the air and catch it again on the string. Jugglers often still use diabolo in their act.

TRIANGLE FOLDS

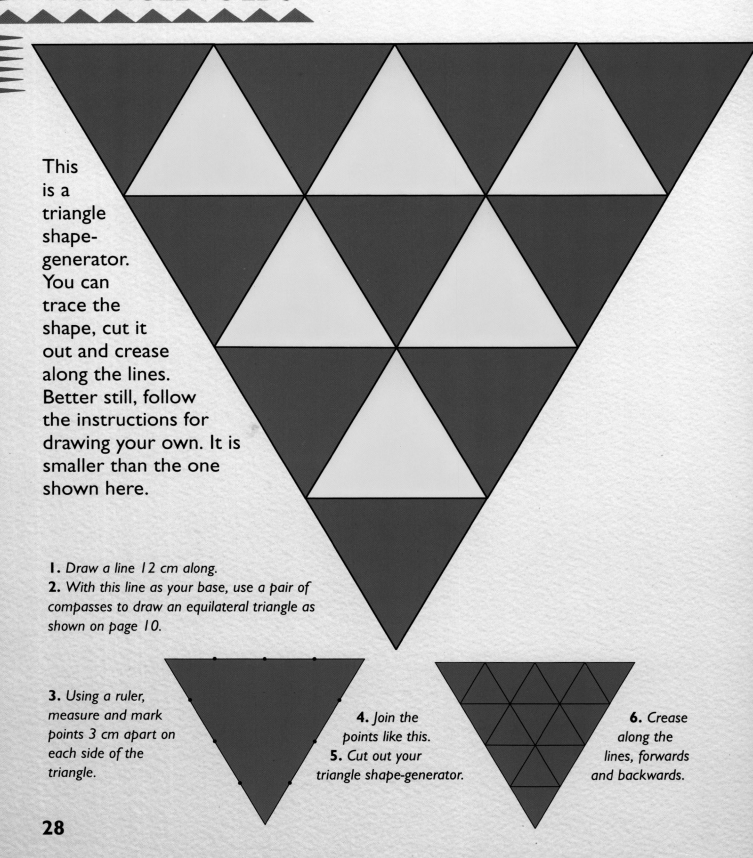

This is a triangle shape-generator. You can trace the shape, cut it out and crease along the lines. Better still, follow the instructions for drawing your own. It is smaller than the one shown here.

1. Draw a line 12 cm along.
2. With this line as your base, use a pair of compasses to draw an equilateral triangle as shown on page 10.

3. Using a ruler, measure and mark points 3 cm apart on each side of the triangle.

4. Join the points like this.
5. Cut out your triangle shape-generator.

6. Crease along the lines, forwards and backwards.

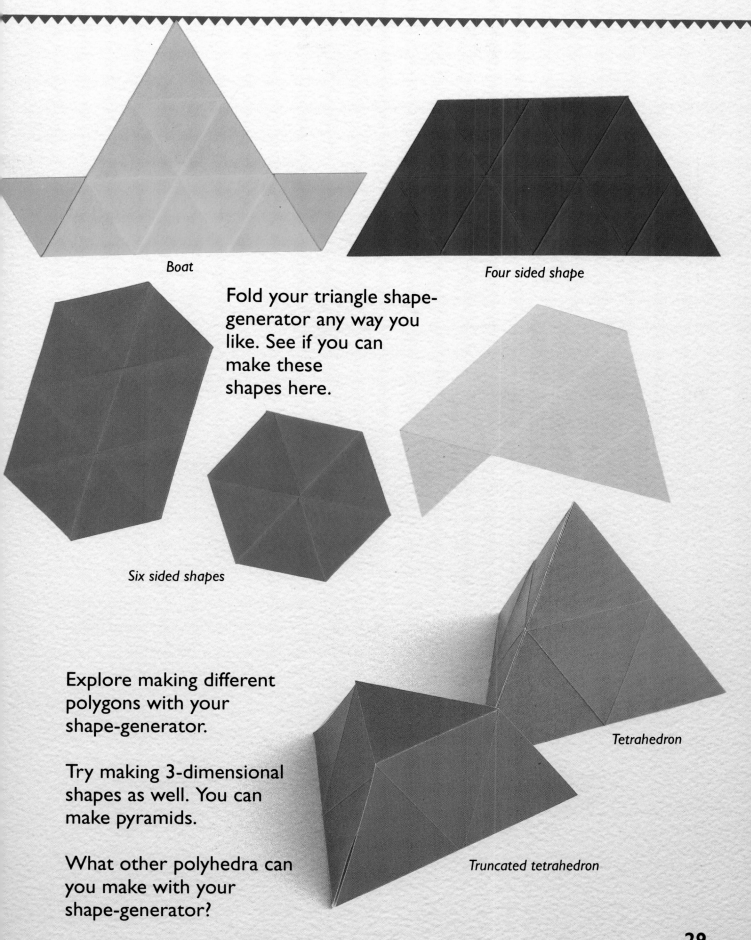

Boat

Four sided shape

Fold your triangle shape-generator any way you like. See if you can make these shapes here.

Six sided shapes

Tetrahedron

Explore making different polygons with your shape-generator.

Try making 3-dimensional shapes as well. You can make pyramids.

What other polyhedra can you make with your shape-generator?

Truncated tetrahedron

GLOSSARY

Acute triangle: a triangle that has all three angles smaller than a right angle. Acute describes any angle that is smaller than a right angle.

Angle: a corner where two straight lines meet. Angles are measured in degrees, which indicate how much of a circle an angle turns through. There are 360 degrees in a complete circle. Another name for an angle is a vertex.

Cone: a 3-D shape which has a circle base and a curved surface coming to a vertex.

Equilateral triangle: a triangle that has all three sides the same length.

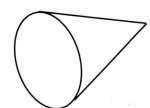

Isosceles triangle: a triangle that has two sides the same length.

Net: a flat or 2-D shape which will fold up to make a 3-D shape.

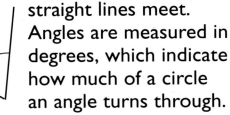

Obtuse triangle: a triangle that has one corner bigger than a right angle. Obtuse describes any angle that is larger than a right angle.

Parallelogram: a 4-sided shape, where opposite sides are parallel, remaining the same distance apart.

Polygon: a 2-D shape which has three or more straight sides. A triangle is a polygon.

Polyhedron: a 3-D shape made from lots of polygons. A pyramid is a polyhedron. More than one polyhedron are called polyhedra.

Protractor: an instrument for measuring the size of an angle in degrees.

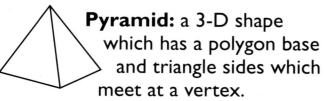

Pyramid: a 3-D shape which has a polygon base and triangle sides which meet at a vertex.

Right angle: the angle formed by a quarter of a complete turn. It measures 90 degrees. A right angle is sometimes called a square corner. A right angled triangle has one right angled corner.

Scalene triangle: a triangle with none of its three sides the same length.

Skeletal shapes: shapes which have edges and corners but no faces, so that you can see right through them.

Symmetrical: a shape or pattern is said to be symmetrical when it can be divided into two parts that reflect each other exactly. This effect is described as mirror symmetry. There are some other kinds of symmetry.

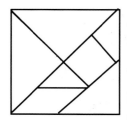

Tangram: a shape which has been cut up into several pieces; the pieces are used to make pictures, shapes and patterns.

Tessellation: fitting shapes together without leaving gaps and without overlapping.

Tetrahedron: a pyramid with four faces, each one a triangle. More than one tetrahedron are called tetrahedra.

Three-dimensional (3-D): describes a shape that has the three dimensions of length, width and depth. A pyramid is an example of three-dimensional shape. A flat shape, such as a triangle, has only length and width so it is called two-dimensional.

Triangle: any 3-sided shape with straight sides.

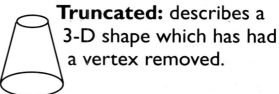

Truncated: describes a 3-D shape which has had a vertex removed.

Vertex: a corner. More than one vertex are called vertices. (See also angle.)

INDEX